Rich Retirement

How to Achieve Financial Success in
Your Golden Years

Table of Contents

Chapter 1. Introduction

Welcome to a journey that promises to transform the twilight of your life into a season of contentment and joy! Our special report, "Rich Retirement: How to Achieve Financial Success in Your Golden Years," is your roadmap to a financially secure future. Crafted with care, this enlightening piece will dissect the complexities of financial management, retirement savings, and fruitful investment strategies. We take a hearty and uplifting approach to this non-technical subject, painting a vision of retirement that is not just about surviving, but thriving! Our ultimate goal is to motivate, inspire, and provide actionable advice. By the end of this unique guide, you'll not only be enticed to purchase it, but also feel empowered to take control of your economic destiny to live out a rich and fulfilling retirement.

Chapter 2. Securing Your Nest Egg: Fundamentals of Retirement Savings

We embark on this instructive journey by delving into the fascinating world of retirement savings. Seeking financial success in the golden years necessitates a vigilant, tactical, and disciplined approach, given the uncertainties associated with future income and expenses.

2.1. Understanding Retirement Savings: The Basics

Fundamentally, retirement savings stand as financial reserves that you systematically instill during your working years to support a lifestyle once earned income ceases. The precise determination of how much should be set aside for retirement is contingent on various factors such as income, expenses, retirement age, life expectancy, and desired lifestyle to name a few.

Factors Influencing Retirement Savings	Brief Explanation
Current Age and Retirement Age	The more years you have until retirement, the more time to save and grow your money.
Income Levels	Higher income levels generally allow for more savings.
Lifestyle Preferences	A luxurious retirement lifestyle necessitates greater savings.
Health and Life Expectancy	Longer life spans require more extensive funding.

Factors Influencing Retirement Savings	Brief Explanation
Inflation	Increases in the cost of living reduce purchasing power, demanding increased savings.

Methodical planning and disciplined execution are imperative to achieving this purpose. Selecting the right savings instruments and expeditiously adjusting to changing circumstances are equally pivotal.

2.2. Retirement Savings Vehicles

There exist varied retirement savings instruments, each boasting unique advantages, restrictions, and tax implications. Your choice should being guided by your particular financial landscape, risk tolerance, and retirement objectives. Let's walk through some common retirement savings vehicles.

- 401(k) Plans: Traditional 401(k) plans offer a tax-deferred growth mechanism, implying that your contributions are made pre-tax, then taxed during withdrawal.

- IRAs: Individual retirement accounts (IRAs) could be traditional or Roth, with the key differentiation lying in the tax-treatment of contributions and withdrawals.

- Defined Benefit Plans: These promise a pre-determined monthly benefit during retirement, typically based on your salary and tenure.

- Defined Contribution Plans: Instead of guaranteeing specific retirement benefits, these set the amounts employees and employers contribute.

- Annuities: Leveraging sizable initial payment or series of payments, annuities guarantee fixed income, generally for the lifespan of the policyholder.

Each of these instruments has its pros and cons. It's important to understand these while creating a diversified retirement portfolio.

2.3. Impact of Diversification

Diversification is a crucial strategy for any investment plan, including retirement savings. By diversifying retirement savings among a variety of assets, one aims to maximize returns and minimize risk. This is because different asset types usually perform differently under various market conditions.

It's crucial to understand — diversification isn't about simply increasing the number of investments, but about strategically choosing a mix of different investment types. This blend is typically decided based on factors like risk tolerance, investment horizon, and retirement financial requirements.

2.4. Consistent Contributions

Another critical aspect of retirement savings is making consistent contributions. The advantage of this approach is twofold: Firstly, consistent contributions average out the cost of acquiring assets over time, a phenomenon referred to as dollar-cost averaging. Secondly, making regular investments also keeps one disciplined and less likely to divert funds meant for retirement savings to other transient needs.

It is advised to begin by saving at least a small amount and then gradually increasing contributions as income rises, or as you find opportunities for savings in your budget.

2.5. Power of Compounding

The power of compounding is another essential element of retirement savings. Through compounding, even modest contributions, if invested consistently over a long period, can accumulate to a sizeable retirement portfolio.

Keep in mind, time is of the essence here. Starting early gives your money more time to grow, allowing more interest to be earned on the interest already accumulated.

2.6. Conclusion

Ensuring financial autonomy in retirement requires earnest effort during one's career. This is to build a nest egg substantial enough to weather unforeseen expenses and maintain a comfortable lifestyle. By comprehending the spectrum of retirement savings basics, taking advantage of common retirement savings instruments, leveraging the virtues of diversification, maintaining consistent contributions, and harnessing the power of compounding, you are in possession of a practical guide to garnering a secure retirement.

As we journey further, we'll delve deeper into each of these components — dissecting their various angles, exploring how to reap maximum benefits, and understanding to tune them to your unique circumstances. Remember, enriching your golden years is not merely a dream — it's a goal that can be achieved through a combination of prudent planning, smart saving, and diligent investing.

Chapter 3. Mastering the Art of Budgeting during Retirement

Understanding financial management during retirement begins with mastering the art of budgeting. Given the limited income or potentially fluctuating investments, devising a functional, yet flexible budget is crucial.

3.1. Understanding Your Income

Start with gaining a comprehensive understanding of your income. In retirement, income often comes from various sources, such as social security, pensions, annuities, part-time employment, and investment returns.

List down the exact monthly amounts received from each source. In case of variable income, such as dividends or returns from investments, count these as a conservative estimate for computing your monthly budget.

Source	Estimated Monthly Income
Social Security	$_
Pension	$_
Retirement Accounts (401k, IRA, etc.)	$_
Investments	$_
Part-time Employment	$_
Annuities	$_

Remember to adjust this number as time moves on to account for increases due to inflation, changes in yields, or modifications in your employment status.

3.2. Identifying Necessary Expenditures

Your retirement budget isn't simply about the income you receive monthly; it's also about how that income is spent. Identify the necessary expenditures versus the discretionary ones.

Essential costs may include:

- Housing (mortgage, rent, property taxes, insurance, maintenance)
- Utilities (electricity, water, heating, telephone, internet)
- Healthcare (insurance premiums, medications, out-of-pocket expenses)
- Food
- Transportation (vehicle maintenance, fuel, insurance, public transport)

Discretionary expenditures might comprise:

- Leisure (travel, hobbies)
- Dining out
- Gifts and charitable donations

Take time to analyse and categorise your spending habits. Do you dine out frequently, or are you content eating at home? Do you wish to loan money to your children or are focused on supporting your retirement only? Do you like traveling or staying put appeals?

It's these personal propensities and priorities that will influence the secondary slice of your budget.

3.3. Constructing the Budget

After having a clear view of your income and expenses, it's time to construct the budget. The objective of this stage is to ensure your income covers your monthly expenses along with leaving room for savings and investments.

Expense	Estimated Monthly Cost
Housing	$_
Utilities	$_
Healthcare	$_
Food	$_
Transportation	$_
Leisure	$_
Dining out	$_
Gifts and Charitable Donations	$_

In case your estimated costs surpass your income, revisit your expenses and work out where cuts can be made.

3.4. Incorporating a Savings Plan into the Budget

A sturdy savings plan is crucial for unforeseen expenses. It can be an emergency medical bill, unplanned travel, sudden home repairs, or a poor run in the stock market. Aim for a savings goal that would cover six months' worth of expenses.

Savings Goal	$_
Current Savings	$_
Monthly Savings Plan	$_

Building a reserve may entail stricter budgeting, less discretionary spending and potentially additional income sources. Remember, these are merely short-term sacrifices for long-term security.

3.5. Regularly Reviewing and Adjusting

Financial landscapes continually morph. The value of investments fluctuates, healthcare costs unexpectedly surge, or a pandemic alters our spending habits irrevocably. The budget you create is not chiselled in stone, but must evolve as your life circumstances transform.

Regularly review your budget, preferably on a quarterly basis. This allows for necessary corrections to ensure you're on the right track. Keep vigilant of your spending habits, cost of living changes, potential health conditions, or volatile market conditions that can impact your income or expenditure.

Mastering the art of budgeting during retirement doesn't have to be daunting. It is an endeavour rooted in a deep understanding of your income and expenses. When shaped thoughtfully and reassessed regularly, your budget becomes a tool empowering you to take control of your economic destiny, leading you towards a fruitful and satisfying retirement, unhindered by financial stress.

Chapter 4. Investment Techniques: Growing Your Wealth After Work

Investing is not about getting rich quickly. It's about securing your future and making your retirement years a time of joy and satisfaction. Being retired doesn't mean that you stop generating wealth. In fact, the opposite is true. You've got various investment techniques at your disposal to grow your wealth after retirement. This section highlights the different ways in which you can invest after retirement for steady growth of your wealth.

4.1. The Power of Diversified Portfolio

When investing, it's important to spread your eggs across different baskets. Diversifying the investment portfolio provides a layer of protection against financial losses. No single investment performs best under all economic conditions and diversification mitigates this risk.

Imagine this: you invested all your retirement funds in high-yield corporate bonds. What happens if there's a glitch in the market, and the corporations issuing the bonds go bankrupt? Your entire investment could go to waste. Diversification provides you with a safety net for such unpredictable scenarios.

Ideally, you should spread your investments over different asset classes: stocks, bonds, real estate, commodities, and even cash. Each asset class responds differently to market conditions and by diversifying, you will average out the losses and gains across your portfolio.

Moreover, within asset classes, opt for further diversification. For instance, don't just buy shares from one sector or one geographical area. Similarly, don't put all your cash in a single savings account with one financial institution. Be as broad as possible in your diversification to spread the risk and maximize the chances of a healthy return on your investment.

4.2. The Dividend Investment Strategy

Another strategy you can use to grow your wealth after work is the dividend investment strategy. This strategy involves investing in companies that pay dividends to their shareholders. The idea is to create a stream of income that you can rely on during your retirement years.

Dividends are portions of a company's profit shared with shareholders and can be a significant source of income - especially for retirees. While not all companies pay dividends, those that do are usually quite stable and financially sound, which adds a layer of security to your investments.

Diminishing the possibility of running out of money is a chief concern for many retirees. Regular dividend income can serve as a financial cushion.

Chapter 5. The Bond Ladder

The bond ladder is another investment strategy that can guarantee you steady income during your retirement years. This strategy involves buying a collection of bonds with varying maturity dates. As one bond matures, the funds are reinvested into a new bond.

A bond ladder can help manage interest rate risk, as you're not locked into a long-term bond that might lose value if interest rates increase. This way, your money is continuously reinvested at current rates.

5.1. The Bucket Investment Strategy

The bucket strategy divides your investment portfolio based on the time frame. The first bucket is for short-term needs, the second for medium-term needs, and the third for long-term needs.

The first bucket should contain safe, liquid investments such as money market funds or short-term bonds to take care of immediate expenses or emergencies. The second bucket is for income-generating investments like dividend-paying stocks, and the third is for growth investments such as equities or real estate.

5.2. Robo-Advisors

In the golden age of technology, consider leaning on Robo-advisors, which can take some of the legwork out of investing. These digital platforms provide automated, algorithm-based investment services without human intervention. They can help you in making more informed investment decisions based on your risk tolerance and goals.

Robo-advisors also allow you to automate your investing, hence eliminating emotional involvement in investment decision-making which often leads to poor financial choices.

5.3. Wrapping Up

Investing after retirement doesn't have to be a daunting task. The key is to focus on building a diversified portfolio that can generate steady income while limiting exposure to unnecessary risks. Whether you're investing in bonds, using a dividend investment strategy, constructing a bond ladder, or using Robo-advisors, the understanding and adoption of these effective strategies can significantly increase your wealth in your golden years.

Remember, it's never too late to start investing. In your retirement years, investing wisely can give you financial freedom, allowing you to fully enjoy the fruits of your labor.

With the insights offered in this guide, we encourage you to take hold of your economic future, transform your twilight into gold, and add richness to your retirement. Your journey to a well-deserved, fulfilling, and financially secure retirement begins today!

Chapter 6. Understanding Your Social Security Benefits

The Social Security system remains one of the most crucial aspects of financial security in retirement in the United States, affecting virtually every American at some point in their lives. From the moment you start your first job until the day you retire, you pay into this system. As such, understanding this structure and its benefits is a key step towards achieving a rich retirement.

6.1. Social Security: A Brief Overview

First, let's understand what Social Security is. Established in 1935 under President Franklin D. Roosevelt, the program was initially created as an insurance plan for aging, unemployed, or disabled workers. Funded through payroll taxes, Social Security benefits are based on your lifetime earnings, adjusting your highest 35 years of wages for inflation. If you've worked fewer than 35 years, the calculation includes zeros for the years you did not work.

6.2. Understanding Your Social Security Statement

Every year, the Social Security Administration (SSA) sends out a comprehensive statement to workers beginning at age 25, covering the benefits that you and your family may be entitled to receive. The statement provides an overview of your estimated benefits at various retirement ages, as well as benefits for disability and survivor benefits for your heirs. It's essential to review this document carefully for any discrepancies or potential errors.

6.3. When to Start Drawing Benefits

You can start receiving Social Security retirement benefits at age 62, but monthly benefits are reduced if you start drawing them before your 'full retirement age.' The full retirement age, depending on your birth year, ranges from 65 to 67. Delaying benefits beyond your full retirement age can increase your monthly compensation up to age 70, as you'll be eligible for 'delayed retirement credits.'

6.4. How Benefits are Calculated

The formula to calculate your benefits at full retirement age takes into account your 35 highest-earning years, indexed for inflation. It gives you 90% of the first $996 (as of 2020) you earned, 32% of earnings between $996 and $6,002, and 15% of any earnings over $6,002. These values are added up to provide a rough average of indexed monthly earnings (AIME).

Your primary insurance amount (PIA) is then determined based on the AIME. The PIA is the foundation of the benefits calculation if you're retiring at your full retirement age.

6.5. Factors That Can Affect Your Benefits

Several factors can impact your Social Security benefits, including:

- Lifetime earnings: The higher your lifetime earnings, the higher your benefits.

- Age at retirement: If you retire early, your benefits will be less than if you wait until full retirement age or later.

- Cost-of-living adjustments (COLA): Every year, the SSA may increase benefits to keep pace with inflation.

- Employment after retirement: If you continue working after starting to receive benefits, it can affect your benefit amount, especially if you're under your full retirement age.

6.6. Maximizing Social Security Benefits

There are a few strategies you can employ to maximize your Social Security benefits:

- Work for at least 35 years: The SSA calculates benefits based on your 35 highest-earning years. If you have not worked 35 years, the SSA will use zeros in the calculation, which can lower your overall benefit amount.

- Boost your income: Higher lifetime earnings equate to higher Social Security benefits.

- Delay claiming: If your health and financial resources allow, delaying the start of your benefits can provide a higher monthly benefit.

- Coordinate with your spouse: Strategies exist for married couples to maximize their benefits together.

Social Security can offer critical support for your retirement goals, but it's not a one-size-fits-all endeavor. By understanding the nuances of the system and your potential benefits, you'll be one step closer to a financially successful golden age!

Chapter 7. Real Estate for Retirement: Proceed with Caution or Dive Right In?

Real estate can be a truly rewarding investment if approached correctly. It can provide a consistent income stream, increase in value over time, and offer tax benefits. However, it does come with its risks, including dealing with property maintenance, problematic tenants, and possible periods of vacancy. Whether this asset class is the right investment for you largely depends on your personal investment goals, the amount of time and effort you're willing to put into property management, and your risk tolerance.

7.1. Understanding the Basics of Real Estate Investing

Before diving into real estate investing, it's crucial to grasp the basics. Real estate encompasses a wide variety of investment types, from residential and commercial properties to land and real estate investment trusts (REITs). Properties can be rented, flipped after renovations, or held onto for their potential appreciation in value.

One key factor in successful real estate investing is location. A property in a thriving area with lots of job growth is likely to appreciate faster than a property in a less desirable area. It's also important to consider other factors like the property's condition, the cost of insurance and property taxes, potential rental income, and your ability to manage the property.

When investing in real estate, you could either put your money in physical properties or properties owned by corporate investors through REITs. Unlike owning a physical property, investing in REITs does not involve getting your hands dirty dealing with renovations, tenant issues or other management tasks.

7.2. Weighing Risks Vs Rewards

While investment in real estate has the potential for significant returns, it also carries inherent risks. These include potential property damage, unexpected expenses, fluctuating market values, problematic tenants, and vacancy periods where the property doesn't generate income. If you have a mortgage on the property, you'll still need to make your monthly payments even during times when the property isn't rented.

When considering investing in real estate, run the numbers thoroughly. Consider all potential costs, including those that may not be immediately apparent, such as maintenance, repairs, and property management fees. Look at the potential income from rent, the property's potential appreciation in value over time, and any tax benefits you may receive.

7.3. Building a Well-Diversified Portfolio

Diversification is a key concept in investing. By spreading investments across various asset classes, you can reduce risk. Therefore, if you decide to invest in real estate, it's important to ensure that your overall investment portfolio remains well-diversified.

Investing too heavily in real estate can increase your risk if the property market takes a downturn. However, having some money in real estate can provide a buffer against volatility in the stock market.

7.4. Leveraging Real Estate Investment Trusts (REITs)

For those looking for a passive way to invest in real estate, consider REITs. A REIT is a company that owns, operates, or finances income-generating real estate. When you invest in a REIT, you're purchasing shares of the company, much like buying stock in any other company.

REITs are legally required to distribute at least 90% of their income to shareholders in the form of dividends. This requirement often results in higher-than-average dividend yields, making them attractive to retirement investors looking for consistent income.

7.5. Doing Your Due Diligence

No matter which path you choose for real estate investing, always do your due diligence. Research the properties or companies in which you're considering investing, run the numbers, and make sure the investment fits within your overall investing strategy.

Remember, investing in real estate for retirement is not a guarantee of wealth. Proceed with caution and dive in only after you've carefully weighed the pros and cons, considered your risk tolerance, and thought about how much time and effort you're willing to put into managing real estate investments.

Chapter 8. Healthcare Expenses: Planning for the Inevitable

One of the most significant concerns for retirees is maintaining a quality, healthy life without depleting their hard-earned savings—a balancing act that requires careful consideration and planning. Let's explore how to navigate these waters successfully.

8.1. Evaluating Your Current Health Status

Understanding your current health and potential future health needs is an essential factor in estimating your healthcare expenses in retirement. This assessment must include regular checkups, medication expenses, and anticipated major treatments. Past medical history and hereditary diseases must also be acknowledged.

You may find assistance from your physician in completing this task. They can help estimate costs for potential future treatments, suggest preventative health measures, and refer you to financial advisors who specialize in healthcare expenses.

8.2. Understanding Medicare and Its Limitations

Medicare is a key benefit for those over 65 in the United States. However, it is important to understand that it does not cover all health expenses. Deductibles, co-pays, prescription medications, and long-term care are some of the significant expenses that Medicare does not cover fully—or at all.

Understanding Medicare Parts A, B, C, and D—their benefits, costs, and gaps—will give you a solid foundation for your healthcare cost planning. Medicare Supplement Insurance (Medigap) can cover some of these gaps and offers a variety of plans that suit a range of needs and budgets.

8.3. Investing in Long-Term Care Insurance

Long-term care (LTC) insurance helps pay for a range of services that aren't covered by standard health insurance or Medicare. These often include assistance with routine daily activities like bathing, dressing, or getting in and out of bed.

The cost of LTC insurance can vary significantly based on coverage type, the age when you buy the policy, and the benefits it provides. Some policies also offer inflation protection, which can be worth considering due to the continuously rising cost of healthcare.

8.4. Preparing for Out-of-Pocket Expenses

One reality of retirement is that out-of-pocket expenses are bound to occur. These costs can range from copayments and coinsurance to medication and treatments not covered by insurance.

It would be best to create a realistic budget that factors in these expenses over the years. It may be wise to annually set aside extra savings specifically for unexpected healthcare costs.

8.5. Factoring in Inflation

As you plan for future medical expenses, it is vital to consider the rising cost of healthcare, which many times outpaces the standard rate of inflation.

Historically, healthcare costs have increased by around 5% annually—an indication that a healthcare dollar today will not go as far in the future. Using this or a similar percentage to adjust projected expenses, you can arrive at a more accurate estimate for your needs.

8.6. Consulting a Professional

Healthcare planning can be complex. Its interdependence with governmental policies, legal frameworks, and financial market conditions may make it necessary to seek advice from experts.

Financial advisors who specialize in retiree healthcare planning can provide personalized understanding and strategies for a secure healthcare future. They can help foresee potential challenges and opportunities related to healthcare inflation, stock market fluctuations, and legislative changes.

8.7. Developing a Healthy Lifestyle

The journey towards retirement is an opportune time to assess and adjust your lifestyle. Adopting healthier habits—such as a balanced diet, regular exercise, and adequate sleep—can contribute to decreasing healthcare needs and expenses.

Remember, investing in your health today can save money on medical costs in the future, not to mention the intangible benefits of enjoying your golden years in good health.

8.8. Conclusion

Failing to plan for healthcare expenses in retirement is, in essence, planning to fail. But with the required knowledge and careful planning, you can confidently face the future, knowing you're closely guarded against crippling healthcare costs. Let these strategies serve as the catalyst toward joy and contentment in your retirement—making the twilight years the best they can possibly be!

Chapter 9. Turning Hobbies into Cash: Creative Ways to Supplement Your Income

Imagine standing on the cusp of retirement, the promise of years filled with personal fulfillment and leisure activities ahead. Many individuals dream of this time, focusing on how they will spend their abundance of free time. However, you have an opportunity to turn this leisure time into a financial advantage. This chapter provides imaginative and practical insights into how one can turn hobbies into streams of income during the golden years.

9.1. Exploring Your Passion

The best starting point before turning your hobby into a source of income is realizing and exploring what you genuinely love doing. Perhaps you enjoy baking, writing, gardening, woodworking, or knitting. These primary hobbies are not just passable times, but they could be your stepping stones towards financial success.

Understanding what you love doing helps align your skills and interests. There's a saying: "Do what you love, and never work a day in your life." When you choose a hobby you like, your passion will drive your perseverance and creativity. One of the greatest benefits that comes from exploring your passion is the satisfaction and fulfillment from doing something you love, while generating an income.

9.2. Assessing Your Skills

After identifying your passion, the next step is to assess your proficiency in that particular hobby. A self-audit can help you determine your expertise level. A hobby's income-generating potential is often proportional to your ability to provide value in the market. For example, if crafting is your hobby, you may want to assess your ability to create unique, high-quality pieces that can compete favorably in the market.

9.3. Market Research

A critical next step in the process of turning your hobby into cash is conducting market research. Determining whether there's a market for your products or services is vital. Use online platforms to begin your research, looking into trends, customer needs, and competition in the space. Comment sections, online reviews, and engaging in forums can provide a wealth of information.

This step helps you understand what the market requires, thus enabling you to polish your craft to meet customers' needs. Consider supplemental courses or workshops that can help bolster your skills where needed, thus positioning you to meet market demands effectively.

9.4. Developing a Business Plan

Once you have refined your skills to meet the demands of the market, it's time to formalize your operations with a business plan. This plan should outline your business' goals, financial needs, marketing strategy, and sustainability plans. For instance, if you plan for your baking hobby to supplement your retirement income, you need to establish how you'll sell your products, price them, and maintain a steady supply to the market.

9.5. Implementing Your Plan

With your business plan in hand, it's now time to set your plan into motion. Invest reasonable resources into your new project, always wary not to jeopardize your financial stability. Start small, possibly testing out your product or service within your local community, then scale up as demand increases.

Use social media and online marketplaces as an inexpensive and effective method to promote your product or service to a broader audience. Collaborate with other hobbyists or small business owners to build a supportive network. Participate in craft fairs, farmers' markets, or local events to showcase your work and build your customer base.

9.6. Wrapping Up: The Promise of a Satisfying Second Career

Transforming your hobby into an additional income source in retirement can promise not only financial success but also personal fulfilment. This process gives an opportunity to further explore your passions, build your skills, and maintain an active lifestyle. It's a satisfying and rewarding "second career" that doesn't feel like a job due to your love and passion for it.

Remember, the journey towards transforming your hobby into cash can be one filled with challenges as well as rewards, but the process of turning your passion into profit can be a fulfilling adventure you look forward to each day of your retirement life.

Ensure to take time to review and adjust your business plan as required, constantly refining your products or services to meet the evolving market needs effectively. Stay open-minded and always ready to learn, as these will position you towards achieving a rich retirement that you've always desired.

Chapter 10. Retirement Accounts Demystified: From IRAs to 401(k)s and Beyond

When it comes to optimizing your retirement savings, it's important to understand the different accounts available to you. From Individual Retirement Accounts (IRAs) to 401(k)s, this chapter will shed light on these plans, their fundamental characteristics, and how to navigate them effectively.

10.1. Understanding Retirement Accounts

At a fundamental level, all retirement accounts function as vehicles for saving and investing, each offering unique benefits in tax advantages, contribution limits, and withdrawal rules. In the end, they all aim at the same target—securing your financial future.

10.2. Individual Retirement Accounts (IRAs)

Two main types of IRAs exist: Traditional and Roth. Both offer tax benefits, but the advantages apply at different stages of the investment process.

Traditional IRAs provide a tax break on contributions. Therefore, each dollar you put into the account reduces your taxable income for that year. The catch? Withdrawals during retirement are taxed as ordinary income.

Roth IRAs, on the other hand, follow a reversed tax structure.

Contributions are taxed normally, but withdrawals during retirement are tax-free. This plan may be more beneficial if you expect your tax rate to be higher during retirement than it is now.

\.Yearly Contribution Limit For IRAs 2022

	Under 50	50 or Older
Traditional IRA	$6,000	$7,000
Roth IRA	$6,000	$7,000

10.3. 401(k) Plans

Employer-sponsored 401(k) plans help workers save and invest for their retirement directly from their paycheck. Traditional 401(k)s operate similarly to traditional IRAs: pre-tax dollars are used for contributions, and distributions are taxed.

However, Roth 401(k)s are an emerging type of plan that adopts the taxation structure of a Roth IRA: post-tax contributions and tax-free withdrawals. Keep in mind, though, not all employers offer Roth 401(k)s.

\.Yearly Contribution Limit for 401(k)s in 2022

	Under 50	50 or Older
Traditional 401(k)	$20,500	$27,000
Roth 401(k)	$20,500	$27,000

10.4. Rollovers

Rollovers occur when you transfer funds from one retirement account to another. Suppose you're changing jobs, for instance. Instead of leaving your 401(k) with your old employer, you might want to rollover those funds into an IRA or your new employer's plan to continue growing your investment.

The key to rollovers is avoiding penalties. If done correctly, you shouldn't incur any taxes or penalties in the process.

10.5. In Conclusion

Knowing the ins and outs of each retirement account can help you make the most of your contributions. Take into account your current tax situation, projected future earnings, and investment goals when deciding which avenue of retirement savings best suits you.

Now that we've demystified these retirement accounts, it becomes easier to draw a map to your golden years. Remember, retirement planning isn't solely about the destination—it's about ensuring the journey is as smooth and stress-free as possible. By understanding and leveraging these retirement options properly, you're just that much closer to a financially successful retirement.

Chapter 11. Decoding the Enigma of Taxes in Retirement

Understanding the various aspects of taxes during retirement can be an enigma. Through this section, we aim to dissect this enigma and present you with lucid, concise, and applicable information.

11.1. Understanding Retirement Taxation

Retirement taxation begins with understanding the tax implications of retirement income. Sources of retirement income typically include Social Security benefits, pension income, withdrawal from tax-deferred accounts like Traditional Individual Retirement Accounts (IRAs), and Return Of Investment from investment portfolios. Each of these sources has its own unique tax rules and implications.

For example, up to 85% of your Social Security benefits may be subject to taxation if you have substantial income apart from Social Security. On the other hand, pensions are generally taxable as ordinary income, which means they are taxed at your regular tax bracket. Withdrawals from tax-deferred accounts like Traditional IRAs are taxed at your marginal tax rate.

It is of utmost importance to recognize these different kinds of income and how they are taxed, as it forms the backbone of tax planning in retirement.

11.2. Your Tax Bracket in Retirement

Generally, you may fall into a lower tax bracket upon retirement because your income is likely to decrease. However, this may not always be true. For instance, if you have a substantial income from investments or your withdrawal from retirement savings is significant, you might find yourselves in a higher tax bracket.

Therefore, understanding your tax bracket is crucial. You need to discern your taxable annual income and then use the IRS Tax Tables to identify your tax bracket. This will give you a perspective on your tax liabilities and allow you to plan accordingly.

11.3. The Roth Advantage

Roth retirement accounts such as Roth IRAs and Roth 401(k)s are unique, as they allow for tax-free withdrawals in retirement. This is because contributions to Roth accounts are made with after-tax dollars. Therefore, withdrawals, including the ones on earnings, are usually free from federal tax, provided certain conditions are met. This provides a significant tax advantage during retirement.

Considering your retirement income sources, it could be beneficial to have a Roth account as part of your retirement portfolio. A balance between taxable and non-taxable sources of income can provide flexibility when it comes to reducing tax liability.

11.4. Tax Deductions and Credits

Just because you're retired doesn't mean you're ineligible for tax deductions and credits. In fact, some deductions might become more significant in retirement. These deductions can reduce your taxable income, thereby lessening your tax burden.

For instance, you can itemize deductions for medical expenses exceeding a certain percentage of your adjusted gross income, an occurrence that tends to be more common in retirement due to higher health care costs. Moreover, you may also qualify for tax credits such as the Credit for the Elderly or Disabled.

It's crucial to acquaint yourself with various deductions and credits appropriate for your circumstances and consult with a tax professional, if necessary.

11.5. Estate Planning and Inheritance Tax

Estate planning is a significant and often overlooked aspect of retirement taxation. Inheritance or estate tax is levied on an individual who inherits or receives a gift. Though many states have abolished this tax, it's crucial to understand your state's inheritance laws and create a proper estate plan that minimizes the tax burden on your beneficiaries.

Remember that the laws governing inheritances are complex and change frequently. Consultation with a tax or estate planning professional will ensure that you understand the latest laws and consequently plan accordingly.

11.6. Be Proactive not Reactive

Possessing knowledge of your retirement tax liabilities allows you to be proactive rather than reactive. The key to tax-efficient retirement lies in being organized and aware. Keep accurate records, understand tax implications, and plan ahead to ensure financial success in your golden years.

Remember, the goal of decoding the enigma of retirement taxation is not to allow taxes to dictate your retirement decisions but to help you make informed and tax-efficient decisions. Make sure to engage a tax professional who can provide assistance tailored to your individual circumstances if need be. Armed with this understanding, you're well on your way to a richer, fulfilling retirement.

Chapter 12. Leaving a Legacy: Estate Planning for Peace of Mind

Creating a comprehensive estate plan is a remarkable stride towards reassuring you of a peaceful and content future, while also ensuring that your cherished assets are passed on to your loved ones in a seamless and tax-efficient manner. But more often than not, we find ourselves stumped when it comes to this crucial aspect of financial management. This stems from a lack of understanding of the subject coupled with the profound emotions attached to it. So, let's calmly steer through the intricacies and nuances of estate planning.

12.1. Understanding Estate Planning

Estate Planning is the methodical approach to organizing one's estate to maximize its benefits for the next generation, reduce taxes, and avoid probate. It encompasses drafting a will, creating trusts, setting up beneficiaries, assigning power of attorney, and even preparing healthcare directives. It's naturally a complex endeavor, requiring thoughtful consideration and professional guidance.

12.2. Importance of Estate Planning

One of the primary misconceptions surrounding estate planning is that it's exclusive to the wealthy. In reality, though, it's applicable to everyone, regardless of the size of your assets. Without an estate plan, decisions regarding your finances could be forced into the hands of a probate court, potentially causing unnecessary expenses and delays. Importantly, estate planning is not just about assets; it also deals with who will take decisions about your healthcare, investments, and even your children's guardianship when you're unable to do so.

12.3. Starting Your Estate Planning

No rule dictates a perfect time to start this process. However, one main component you'd need to instigate your estate planning is a 'will'. It lays out the distribution of your property upon your demise and designates guardians for minor children. A badly drafted or outdated will can lead to family disputes and long legal battles so ensure it's updated and validated regularly.

12.4. Harnessing Trusts in Estate Planning

A trust serves as an excellent tool for giving you control over your wealth even after death. They can help reduce estate taxes and protect your assets from creditors and lawsuits. Living trusts are a popular choice because they avoid probate, allowing for quicker distribution of assets to beneficiaries. However, setting up a trust is complex and may require legal guidance.

12.5. Power of Attorney

This legal document assigns an individual, known as an attorney-in-fact, the authority to handle your affairs when you're unable. You can have a Power of Attorney (POA) for healthcare (making medical decisions on your behalf) or a durable POA for financial matters.

12.6. Choosing Beneficiaries

Part of your estate plan will involve choosing who gets what. You'll list beneficiaries for your individual assets like retirement accounts, insurance policies, and investments, and you can even specify percentages for them.

12.7. Estate Tax

Estate tax laws are complex territory, and when not navigated correctly, can levy hefty costs on your heirs. Positioning your assets and estate in a tax-efficient manner prevents your beneficiaries from getting a smaller share due to heavy tax deductions.

12.8. Reviewing and Updating Your Plan

Ensure you periodically review and update your estate plan. Significant life events like the birth of a child, marriage, divorce, or even changes in tax laws could cause a need to amend your plan.

Estate planning can be intensive and emotionally charged. But remember, its primary purpose is to provide for and protect your loved ones. Implementing a solid estate plan, while challenging, ultimately leads to a sense of tranquility knowing that whatever you've worked for will be passed down precisely and efficiently, just as you'd wish it to be.

www.ingramcontent.com/pod-product-compliance
Lightning Source LLC
Chambersburg PA
CBHW072222290526
45794CB00007B/2853

*9 7 9 8 8 5 8 3 2 0 6 9 2 *